# My
# Magical
# Oasis

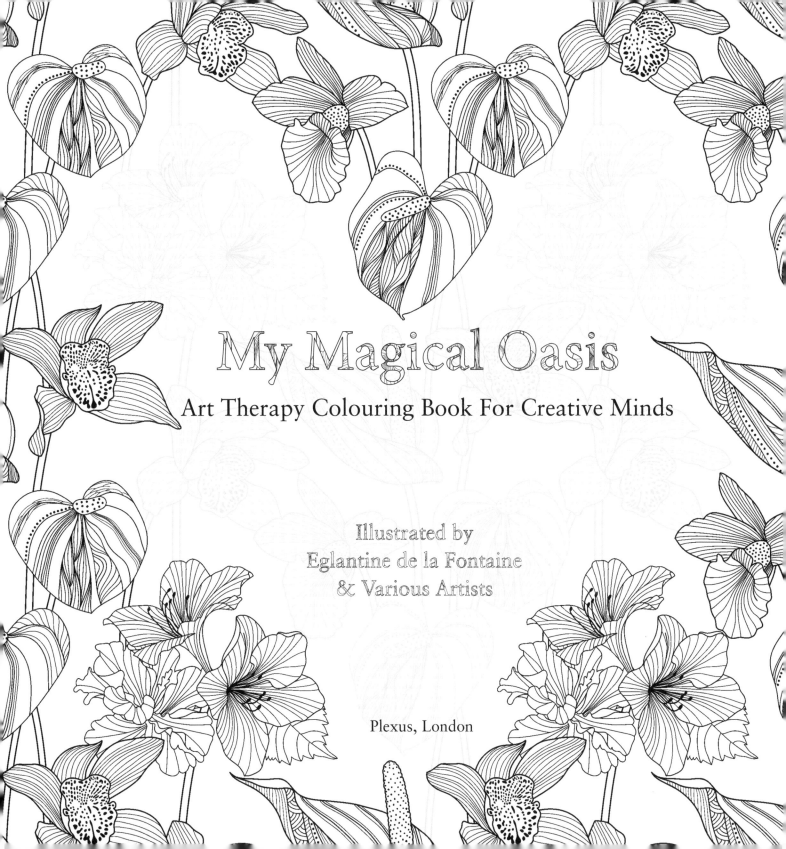

# My Magical Oasis

## Art Therapy Colouring Book For Creative Minds

Illustrated by
Eglantine de la Fontaine
& Various Artists

Plexus, London

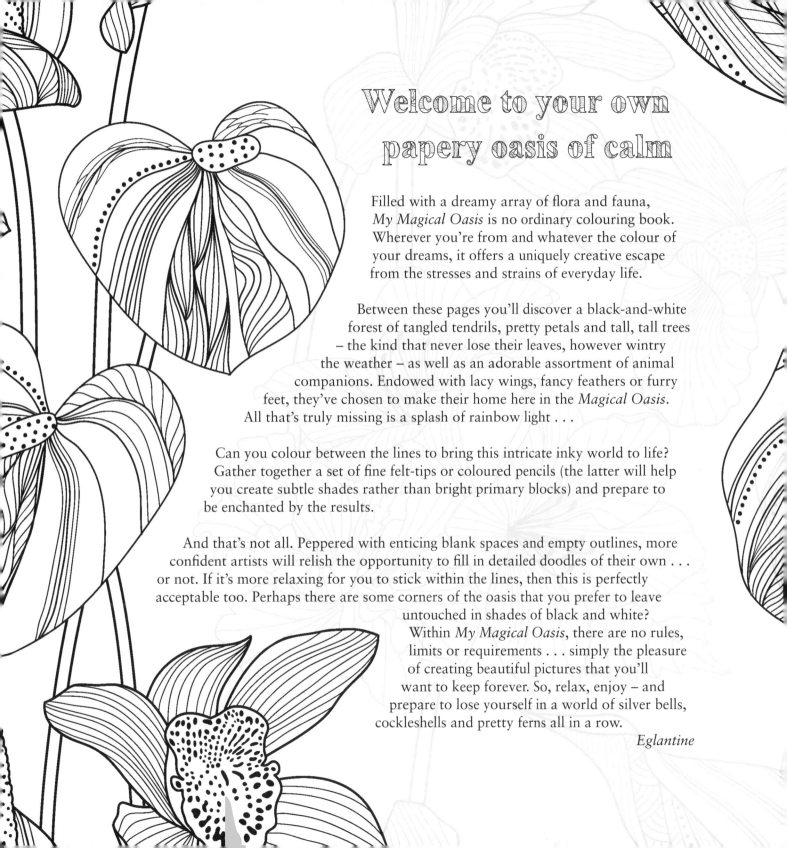

# Welcome to your own papery oasis of calm

Filled with a dreamy array of flora and fauna, *My Magical Oasis* is no ordinary colouring book. Wherever you're from and whatever the colour of your dreams, it offers a uniquely creative escape from the stresses and strains of everyday life.

Between these pages you'll discover a black-and-white forest of tangled tendrils, pretty petals and tall, tall trees – the kind that never lose their leaves, however wintry the weather – as well as an adorable assortment of animal companions. Endowed with lacy wings, fancy feathers or furry feet, they've chosen to make their home here in the *Magical Oasis*. All that's truly missing is a splash of rainbow light . . .

Can you colour between the lines to bring this intricate inky world to life? Gather together a set of fine felt-tips or coloured pencils (the latter will help you create subtle shades rather than bright primary blocks) and prepare to be enchanted by the results.

And that's not all. Peppered with enticing blank spaces and empty outlines, more confident artists will relish the opportunity to fill in detailed doodles of their own . . . or not. If it's more relaxing for you to stick within the lines, then this is perfectly acceptable too. Perhaps there are some corners of the oasis that you prefer to leave untouched in shades of black and white? Within *My Magical Oasis*, there are no rules, limits or requirements . . . simply the pleasure of creating beautiful pictures that you'll want to keep forever. So, relax, enjoy – and prepare to lose yourself in a world of silver bells, cockleshells and pretty ferns all in a row.

*Eglantine*

Fill in fabulous flora to make these parakeets feel at home.

How might these botanical beauties bloom across the page? Use this space for dreamy doodles.

Fill this page with as many tangled tendrils as you'd wish for.

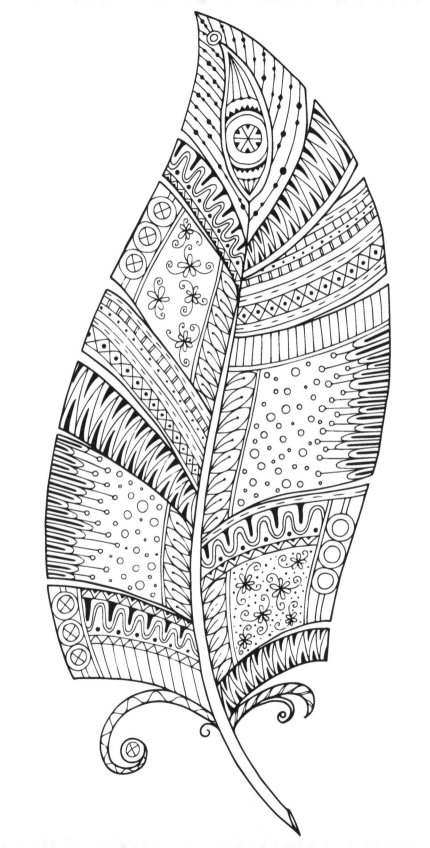

Trace lacy new wings for these two butterflies.

Create a background to match this floral fancy.

Add detail to these delicate dragonfly wings. Doodle more friends to fly with them.

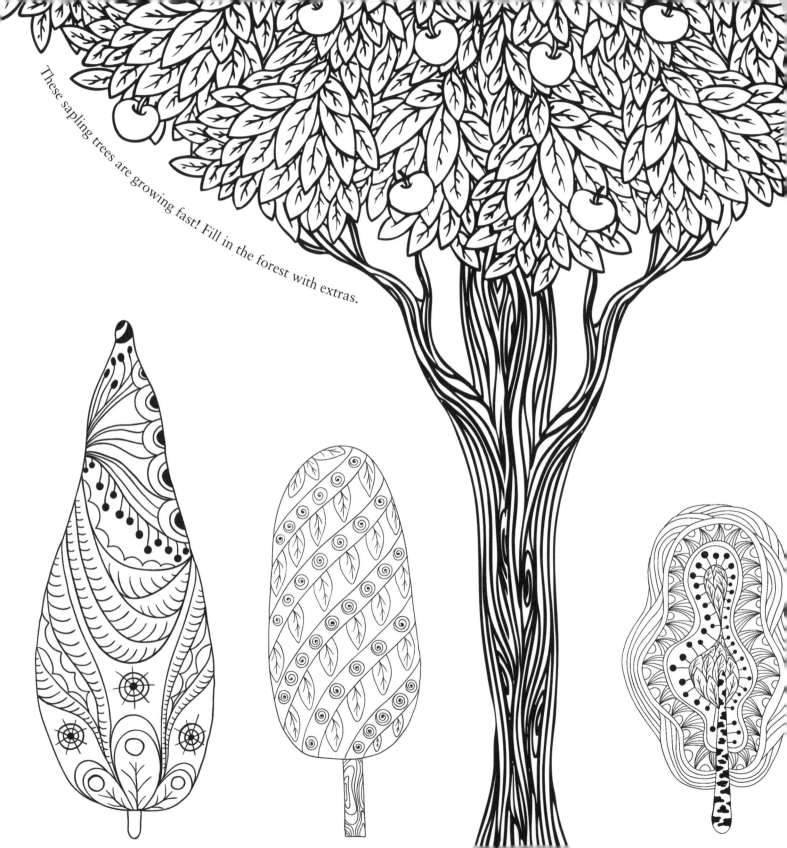

These sapling trees are growing fast! Fill in the forest with extras.

Add patterns to perfect these delicate white petals.

Fill this space with a flurry of winged beauties.

Complete this exotic paradise with blooms and detail of your own.

Sketch more sweetly scented flowers that the butterflies will adore

Use this space to map out the garden of your dreams . . . no watering required.

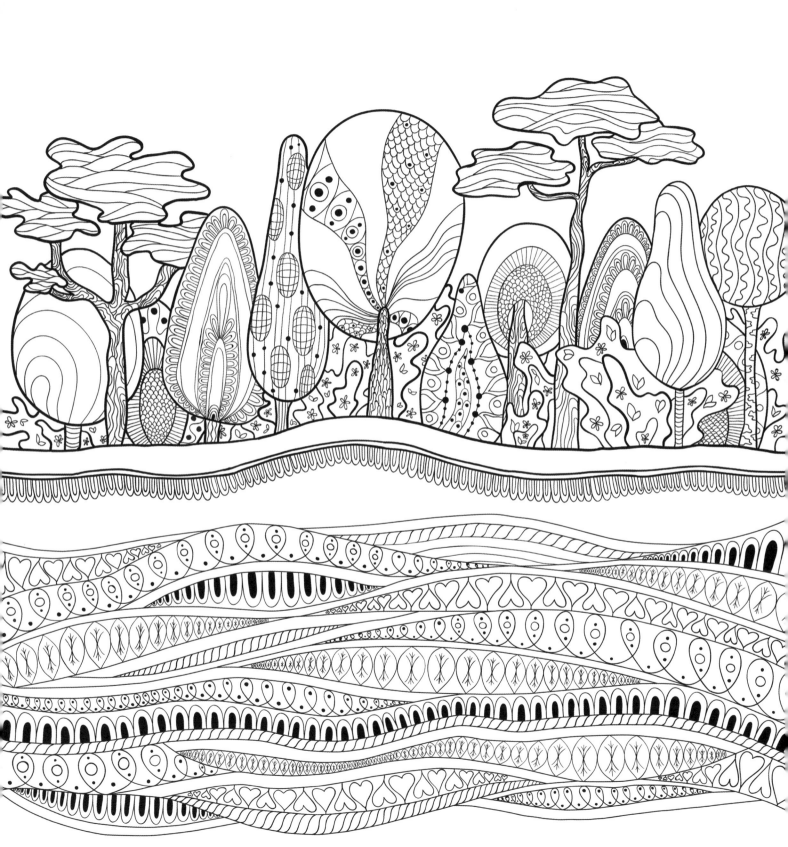

Add patterns to make each and every leaf unique

Birds of a feather flock together – why not add more here?

Fill in the shell of this baby turtle to match her mother.

Add a little extra detail to make these exotic beauties shine.

Add a few extra frills to turn these plain-but-pretty cabbage whites into lovely painted ladies.

Drift along with these soft white clouds as you fill in extra fluffy detail.

British Library Cataloguing in Publication Data
A catalogue record for this book is available
from the British Library

ISBN-13: 978-0-85965-535-4

Illustrations by Eglantine de la Fontaine & various artists
Cover design by Coco Balderrama
Book design by Coco Balderrama
Printed in Great Britain by Bell & Bain Ltd, Glasgow

Thanks to Laura Coulman and April James.
With additional material adapted from www.shutterstock.com

Forthcoming title: My Floral Wonderland